ECONOMICS OF ENTERTAINMENT

THE ECONOMICS OF MAKING A MOVIE

Robin Johnson

 Crabtree Publishing Company

www.crabtreebooks.com

Author: Robin Johnson

Editor-in-chief: Lionel Bender

Editors: Simon Adams, Rachel Eagen

Proofreaders: Laura Booth, Wendy Scavuzzo

Project coordinator: Kathy Middleton

Design and photo research: Ben White

Cover design: Margaret Amy Salter

Production: Kim Richardson

Print and production coordinator:
    Margaret Amy Salter

Prepress technician: Margaret Amy Salter

Consultant: Laura Ebert, Ph.D., Lecturer in
Economics at the State University of New York
at New Paltz, N.Y.

This book was produced for
Crabtree Publishing Company by
Bender Richardson White.

Photographs and reproductions:
Dreamstime.com: 20–21 (Edward Fielding), 21 top (Maxym022), 22–23 Large
(Edward Fielding), 25 top right (Paul Mckinnon), 33 top right (Jborzicchi), 34–
35 (Jabiru), 38 Top (Vvuls), 38–39 bottom large (Xarch009). Getty Images:
12–13 (Dave M. Benett). Shutterstock.com: cover-center (Fotomicar), cover-
middle left inset (Faiz Zaki), cover-bottom left inset (jfreeman), cover-bottom
right inset (Joe Seer), banners (Ferenc Szelepcsenyi), icons (James Steidl,
Texelart, kurhan, Stephen Mcsweeny, R. Gino Santa Maria, graphit, bioraven,
Alex Staroseltsev, sjgh, Olga Rutko), 1 bottom middle (riekephotos), 10–11
(bannosuke), 11 left middle (Regien Paassen), 17 bottom right (Dave
Azoulay), 18–19 (Canadapanda), 26–27 Top Angela Harburn), 28–29
(gary718), 30–31 (Monkey Business Images), 32–33 (cinemafestival), 36–037
(egd), 37 top left (mangostock), 42–43 (Michael Winston Rosa). Science Photo
Library: 26–27 bottom (C.S. LANGLOIS, Publiphoto Diffusion). Topfoto: 4–5
(Warner Bros), 6–7 (United Archives), 8–9 (The Granger Collection), 14–15
(ImageWorks), 16–17, 24–25 (Spike Watson/ArenaPAL), 40–41. Thinkstock:
cover-top, top right inset
Walt Disney, Marvel, NFL, NHL, NBA, MLB, Paramount, Universal, iTunes,
Lionsgate, Warner Brothers, and other manufacturers and brands are
registered trademarks and/or protected by copyright and usually given with
™, ®, or © symbol.

Graphics: Stefan Chabluk

Library and Archives Canada Cataloguing in Publication

Johnson, Robin (Robin R.), author
       The economics of making a movie / Robin Johnson.

(Economics of entertainment)
Includes index.
Issued in print and electronic formats.
ISBN 978-0-7787-7971-1 (bound).--ISBN 978-0-7787-7976-6 (pbk.).--
ISBN 978-1-4271-7870-1 (pdf).--ISBN 978-1-4271-7985-2 (html)

       1. Motion picture industry--Economic aspects--Juvenile
literature. 2. Motion pictures--Production and direction--Juvenile
literature. 3. Motion pictures--Distribution--Juvenile literature.
I. Title.

PN1994.5.J65 2014   j791.43   C2013-907573-9
                                            C2013-907574-7

Library of Congress Cataloging-in-Publication Data

Johnson, Robin (Robin R.)
  The economics of making a movie / Robin Johnson.
       pages cm. -- (Economics of entertainment)
  Includes index.
  ISBN 978-0-7787-7971-1 (reinforced library binding) -- ISBN
978-0-7787-7976-6 (pbk.) -- ISBN 978-1-4271-7870-1 (electronic
pdf) -- ISBN 978-1-4271-7985-2 (electronic html)
1. Motion pictures--Production and direction--Juvenile
literature. 2. Motion pictures--Economic aspects--Juvenile
literature. I. Title.

  PN1995.9.P7J64 2014
  791.4302'3--dc23
                                            2013043399

Crabtree Publishing Company

www.crabtreebooks.com   1-800-387-7650

Printed in Canada/022014/MA20131220

Published in Canada
Crabtree Publishing
616 Welland Ave.
St. Catharines, ON
L2M 5V6

Published in the United States
Crabtree Publishing
PMB 59051
350 Fifth Avenue, 59th Floor
New York, New York 10118

Published in the United Kingdom
Crabtree Publishing
Maritime House
Basin Road North, Hove
BN41 1WR

Published in Australia
Crabtree Publishing
3 Charles Street
Coburg North
VIC, 3058

CONTENTS

THE DREAM FACTORY

Quiet on the set! Roll cameras! And … action! The Hollywood actors and actresses play their parts while the crew captures every scene on film. Soon the movie will be playing at a theater near you. Did you ever wonder how it got there? How much did it cost to make? Who paid for it? Did they make money? And why is movie popcorn so expensive? It all comes down to economics.

Film studies in the United Kingdom made magic in *Harry Potter and the Deathly Hallows, Parts 1 and 2,* starring actor Daniel Radcliffe.

PRODUCERS AND CONSUMERS

Economics is the study of how society decides what and how much to produce, how to produce these goods and services, and for whom to produce them. People use money and other resources to make goods and deliver services. A resource is anything—such as trees, machines, and workers—that is used to produce goods. Filmmakers need scripts, costumes, lights, and cameras to make their goods (movies). What other resources do they need?

Filmmakers also need millions and millions of dollars to make and sell movies. In the film industry, a producer is the person who gets the money to make a movie and who manages every step of the process. In economics, a producer is anyone who uses resources to make goods. **Consumers** are the people who buy and use the goods. When you spend your allowance to see the latest movie, you are a consumer. When you buy a big tub of popcorn to eat at the movies, you become an even bigger consumer. You also become part of the **economy**.

ONE OF A KIND

Hollywood is sometimes called "The Dream Factory." It is a magical place where stars are made and dreams can come true. Like other factories, Hollywood makes products. A product is an item or service that is bought or used by a consumer, such as a movie, a car, or a can of beans. Unlike most industrial factories, however, Hollywood **studios** can spend many years and millions of dollars to make a single, unique product—a movie. Can you imagine spending all that time and money to make just one car or a can of beans?

SHOW BUSINESS

A MULTI-BILLION-DOLLAR INDUSTRY

There's no business like show business! Making movies is a one-of-a-kind, multi-billion-dollar industry—and risky business. Studios are always fighting one another for ticket sales. **Competition** is an economic battle between companies (studios) to sell their products (movies). Studios spend fortunes trying to make bigger and better films each year. They hire the best stars and use clever special effects to lure viewers into theaters. They hope that their films will be **box office** smashes. But no one can predict which films will be hits—or misses.

Hollywood is part of a **market economy**. In a market economy, producers can choose how they spend their money making films and other products. Studios can decide which films to make and how much to **invest** in them. But consumers also have choices. When you use your allowance, you have the freedom to decide how you want to spend it. You stand outside the theater and study the posters. Which film will you see today? The sci-fi adventure flick or the goofball comedy? Or maybe the superhero **sequel**? The choice is up to you.

OUTSIDE THE BOX OFFICE

Studios compete to bring crowds to the box office. But there is also competition for your money outside the movie theater. You can go to theme parks or sporting events or bowling. You choose how to spend your free time and money. Most families have limited **disposable income**. Disposable income is money that is left over after taxes and bills have been paid. It is "fun money" that can be used for leisure activities or movies and other forms of entertainment.

INSIDER INSIGHT

"Nowadays it seems more and more like the 'business' in 'show business' is underlined . . . and it's all part of getting people in to see the movies."
Jeff Bridges, actor

Marvel's The Avengers was the top movie of 2012, selling nearly 80 million tickets in North America alone. It made more than U.S. $1.5 billion in that year.

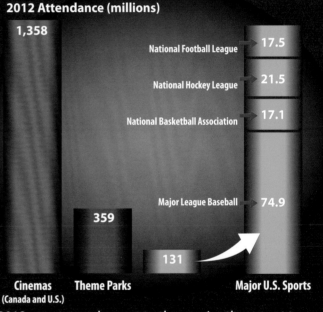

2012 ATTENDANCE AT THE MOVIES

2012 Attendance (millions)

1,358

National Football League — 17.5

National Hockey League — 21.5

National Basketball Association — 17.1

Major League Baseball — 74.9

359

131

| Cinemas (Canada and U.S.) | Theme Parks | Major U.S. Sports |

In 2012, more people went to the movies than went to theme parks and sporting events combined.

HISTORY OF FILM

The first moving picture shows, or "movies," were made in 1895 by Louis and Auguste Lumière. The French brothers had no idea how big their little movies would become. In fact, Louis Lumière famously said, "The cinema is an invention without a future."

Dorothy took viewers over the rainbow and into a world of color in the 1939 movie *The Wizard of Oz*.

DIRECTOR

TRICKS OF THE TRADE

Filmmakers will do just about anything to get people into theaters. In 1960, they introduced Smell-O-Vision to the world. Odors were piped into theaters so audiences could smell the movies! It cost a lot to equip theaters for scented films, however, and the stinky idea soon blew over.

FILM TIMELINE

Late 1800s: Thomas Edison and other inventors develop moving picture cameras.

1895: Brothers Louis and Auguste Lumière make and show the first movies in Paris, France. They are short, silent, black-and-white films.

1905: Small theaters—called nickelodeons—open across America. Viewers pay five cents to see short films. By 1908, there are about 9,000 movie theaters in the country.

1912: Universal Studios begins making movies. It is the first studio in the United States.

1927: The Jazz Singer becomes the first feature film with spoken words. Other talking pictures—called "talkies"—quickly become popular.

1930: About 80 million people—or 65% of the population—go to the movies in the United States each week.

1932: A Walt Disney short cartoon becomes the first full-color film. Other Technicolor films like The Wizard of Oz and Gone with the Wind soon follow.

1933: Movie theaters begin selling refreshments.

1950s: Television becomes popular and draws viewers away from theaters. In the 1960s, nearly every house in America has a "home screen."

1961: A feature film is shown on a commercial airplane for the first time.

1973: Computer-generated imaging (CGI) is used for the first time in the film Westworld.

1975: Jaws becomes the first big blockbuster film.

1992: Three-quarters of homes in the United States have VCRs. Americans spend $12 billion on videos and less than $5 billion at movie theaters.

1995: Pixar releases Toy Story, the first fully computer-animated feature film.

2000: About 27 million people—less than 10% of the population—go to the movies in America each week.

2002: Director George Lucas shoots Star Wars Episode II: Attack of the Clones, the first feature film made with a high-definition digital camera.

2009: Avatar becomes the biggest money-making film in history, earning nearly $3 billion around the world.

2012: There are nearly 40,000 movie screens in the United States. The average ticket price is $7.96.

GET SHORTY

Early cinemas showed silent black-and-white films that lasted about 45 seconds. That's shorter than previews you see in theaters today! The films featured real people leaving a factory, eating breakfast, watering their garden, and doing other simple activities. There were no explosions or car chases. There were no superheroes or vampires. There wasn't even sound or color! Yet audiences fell in love with the new moving pictures.

TALKIES AND TECHNICOLOR

The first talking picture show, The Jazz Singer, hit the big screen in 1927. Other "talkies" soon followed. These new films really got people talking—and rushing—to theaters. In 1930, about 80 million people (about two-thirds of the population at that time) went to the movies each week! Over time, the film industry continued to grow and change. Technicolor was added to films in the 1930s. Movies such as The Wizard of Oz and Gone with the Wind became full-color smash hits. In the 1950s, 3D films began popping up in American theaters. In the 1970s, computer-generated imaging (CGI) brought popular films such as Jaws and Star Wars to life.

Today, new technology keeps consumers coming back to the movies. Think of the last film you saw in a theater. Did you go to see the amazing special effects and computer animation on the big screen? Did you wear 3D glasses and dodge bombs as they exploded around you? Movies have come a long way since the early days of cinema.

HOORAY FOR HOLLYWOOD!

CALIFORNIA—THE CENTER OF THE MOVIE WORLD

Hooray for Hollywood! Hollywood is an area of Los Angeles, California. Major movie studios set up shop there in the early 1900s, and people have been shooting films there ever since. Hundreds of movies are made in Hollywood each year, and theaters sell billions of tickets to see the films. In 2012, there were nearly 1.4 billion movie tickets sold in the United States and Canada alone! You might think that because so many tickets are sold for so many movies and, as ticket prices rise each year, that film studios would always make a **profit**. Profit is the money left over after costs have been paid by the **revenue** (or money) the film brought in.

RISING COSTS

But movies do not always turn a profit. Why not? After all, movie tickets are a lot more expensive today than when movies first came out. Ticket prices are high because the cost of making movies has gone up. The continual rise in the cost of resources and goods is called **inflation**. Every expense—from cameras and lights to actors' **salaries**—has increased. So higher ticket prices do not necessarily mean higher profits. Studios are also spending more and more money on costly special effects to get consumers into theaters. But the special effects have special prices. The 3D film *Avatar* took years and a whopping $237 million to make! Moviegoers pay **premiums**, or extra costs, to see 3D films. But studios still have to sell a ton of tickets and other products to bring in enough revenue to turn a profit.

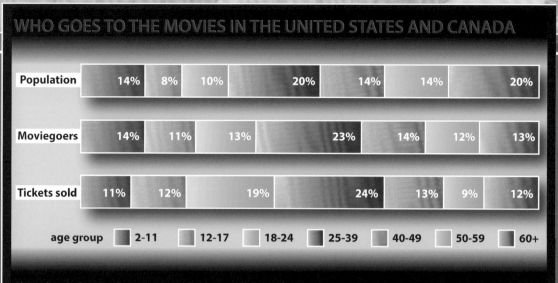

WHO GOES TO THE MOVIES IN THE UNITED STATES AND CANADA

	2-11	12-17	18-24	25-39	40-49	50-59	60+
Population	14%	8%	10%	20%	14%	14%	20%
Moviegoers	14%	11%	13%	23%	14%	12%	13%
Tickets sold	11%	12%	19%	24%	13%	9%	12%

age group ▢ 2-11 ▢ 12-17 ▢ 18-24 ▢ 25-39 ▢ 40-49 ▢ 50-59 ▢ 60+

This chart shows the age breakdown of the population and of those who go to the movies.

LEFT: India has the biggest film industry in the world. It is nicknamed "Bollywood" after California's famous town. Moviegoers flock to theaters such as this one in Jaipur. BELOW: The U.S. film industry is known simply as "Hollywood."

2 GETTING READY TO ROLL

Work on a film begins long before it hits theaters. In the pre-production stage, every detail of the film is carefully planned. Producers must find a script and skilled people to make the movie. They must scout locations and get sets built. Most importantly, they must **finance** the film. Financing is getting **capital**, or money, to make or do something. Without money, the film—no matter how good the script is—will never get made.

MARKET SHARE OF TOTAL TICKET SALES IN 2012

Based on a Fairy Tale or Legend
4 movies 2.81%

Based on a TV Show 9 movies 2.37%

Based on a Factual Book or Article
17 movies 3.01%

Other 19 movies 4.39%

Based on Real Life Events
169 movies 3.43%

Original Screenplay
368 movies 39.74%

Based on a Comic or Graphic Novel
9 movies 14.30%

Based on a Fiction Book or Short Story
85 movies 29.95%

Movies using an original screenplay or that were based on a novel or short story dominated screens in 2012.

Fans of the *Twilight* movies go wild as actors appear at the U.K. premiere, or first showing, of *The Twilight Saga: Breaking Dawn, Part 1* in November 2011.

THE RIGHT STUFF

The first step in pre-production is finding a tale to tell. A film script, or screenplay, is a written work that tells a movie's story. It has all the dialogue, actions, and instructions for the film. Some scripts are original stories. Others are based on books, plays, comics, or television shows. Studios buy scripts from screenwriters.

Studios must also buy the **rights** to the story. Rights are permission to use a story and/or character. Once a studio owns the rights to a story, no other studio can tell the same story or use the same characters. This gives the studio a **monopoly** on the story. A monopoly is when there are many buyers (in this case moviegoers) and only one seller (the movie studio). Having a monopoly allows studios to pour millions of dollars into a movie without worrying that another studio will make the same film.

THE SURE THING

The cost of original scripts starts at about $35,000. Scripts written by well-known screenwriters can cost millions of dollars. Buying the rights to bestselling books or comics can cost even more! Producers are willing to pay top dollar for the story rights, however. They know that popular books— such as *Harry Potter, Twilight,* and *The Hunger Games*—have die-hard fans. The fans will gladly pay to see their favorite wizards and werewolves brought to life on the big screen. Readers of comic books—such as *Spider-Man, Batman,* and *Superman*—will fly into theaters to see their favorite superheroes. Having a built-in fan base takes some of the **risk** out of making high-cost movies.

WHAT DO YOU THINK?

Look at the chart on the opposite page. How many of the films shown in 2012 were based on screenplays? How many were based on comics? What was their **market share**?

SHOW ME THE MONEY!

FINANCING A MOVIE

Besides a script and story rights, a producer needs a director and cast members. Popular actors and directors are **assets** to a movie. An asset is a resource that has economic value or can be turned into cash. Well-known actors and directors bring in revenue for the studios. If famous actors and directors have signed on to make a film, producers are more likely to get the film financed.

Producers get money for their movies from banks, governments, **sponsors**, private **investors**, and any other sources they can find. An investor is someone who contributes money or services to a project in the hope that they will someday make money from it. Many films are financed by big Hollywood studios. Studios are movie-making companies with large buildings and outdoor spaces for shooting films. They plan, produce, and **distribute** movies. Distribution is the costly process of getting films into theaters.

BASIC ECONOMICS

Not all movies are made by big Hollywood studios. Small production companies make independent or "indie" films. Independent filmmakers have more control over their movies but much less money and other resources to make them. Indie movies are often shown at film festivals. A film festival is where movies are watched and sometimes bought by major studios for distribution.

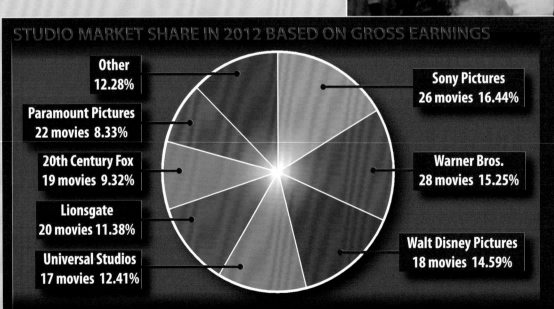

STUDIO MARKET SHARE IN 2012 BASED ON GROSS EARNINGS

Other
12.28%

Paramount Pictures
22 movies 8.33%

20th Century Fox
19 movies 9.32%

Lionsgate
20 movies 11.38%

Universal Studios
17 movies 12.41%

Sony Pictures
26 movies 16.44%

Warner Bros.
28 movies 15.25%

Walt Disney Pictures
18 movies 14.59%

Seven major Hollywood studios dominated the movie market in 2012. Other studios gained just over 12 percent of the total share.

THE BIG SEVEN

Hollywood studios have been making motion pictures for more than 100 years. Today, the top Hollywood studios are Sony Pictures, Warner Bros., Walt Disney Pictures, Universal Studios, Lionsgate, 20th Century Fox, and Paramount Pictures. Together, these seven studios captured nearly 90 percent of the market share in 2012. The chart opposite is based on the **gross** earnings of the top studios. In economics, gross does not mean disgusting (although the money that Hollywood studios earn might make some people sick!). Gross is the total revenue before any costs have been paid.

Riders relive the terror of the 1975 movie *Jaws* at Universal Studios theme park in Orlando, Florida. Theme parks are another source of income for studios.

MOVIE BUDGETS

PLANNED IN DETAIL

Before filming can begin, the producer must make a **budget**. A budget is a detailed plan of how much money will be spent on which items. You may have heard your parents say that you can't go to the movies or buy a new DVD because it's not in the budget. That means that it's not part of the spending plan for that week or month. Many families set a budget to make sure they have enough money to pay their bills. There may be enough room in the budget for movies and other entertainment.

ABOVE AND BELOW

Like parents, film producers plan how every dollar of their budget will be spent. The only difference is that most movie budgets are millions of dollars! Film budgets are broken down into two parts. "Above-the-line" expenses are all the costs of the creative talent. They include salaries for screenwriters, producers, actors, directors, and other people who help shape the story. These are **fixed costs** that do not usually change once filming

BUDGET FOR *SPIDER-MAN 2* (approx. figures)

Production Budget for *Spider-Man 2*

Script: $10 million

Story Rights: $20 million

Producers: $15 million

Director: $10 million

Cast: $30 million

Production Costs: $45 million

Special Effects: $65 million

Music: $5 million

TOTAL BUDGET = $200 MILLION

BUDGET FOR *EL MARIACHI* (approx. figures)

Production Budget for *El Mariachi*

Film Stock: $2,329

Film Processing: $1,323

Equipment (clip-on lamps and bulbs): $127

Acting Fees: $225

Other Production Costs (fake blood, used guitar case, etc.): $397

Video Transfer: $2,824

TOTAL BUDGET = $7,225

begins. "Below-the-line" expenses are all the direct costs of shooting the film. They include crew members, equipment, transportation, building sets, and renting locations. These are **variable costs** that can change during filming. For example, if a scene is cut from the script, the producers will not have to pay the crew to shoot that scene.

BIG AND SMALL

Big Hollywood movies have big budgets. The average studio film costs about $140 million to make. Some movies cost much more. The 2012 film *John Carter* cost at least an incredible $300 million! Independent films such as *El Mariachi* have much smaller budgets. They usually range from a few thousand to a few million dollars.

LEFT: *Spider-Man* movies have supersized budgets.
BELOW: A small crew shoots a low-budget independent film.

MAKING THE MOVIE

Once a movie has been planned and financed, it's time to get the cameras rolling! The production stage is when a movie is filmed. Depending on the budget, shooting a feature film can take weeks, months, or even years. Most studio films take two to six months to shoot. And costs pile up every step of the way.

Movie fans tussle for photos and autographs of U.K. actor Benedict Cumberbatch at the showing of his film *12 Years a Slave* at the Toronto International Film Festival in September 2013.

SHOOTING STARS

One of the biggest costs in making a movie is paying for the cast. Hollywood stars bring loyal fans into theaters and boost ticket sales around the world. But they don't come cheap. Big-name actors and actresses command big salaries. It is not uncommon for a popular actor to earn $20 to $30 million for a starring role in a Hollywood film. Stars also get costly **perks** such as private jets, limos, posh trailers, personal trainers and chefs, acting coaches, and security guards.

GOLDEN OPPORTUNITY

Are the high costs of Hollywood stars worth it? Having a famous actor in a movie is usually worth the expense because of other monetary benefits the star brings to the film. The **opportunity cost**—that is the value of the option that was *not* chosen—is lower if a famous actor is chosen than it would be if an unknown actor was chosen, even if the unknown actor gets paid much less.

For example, say a studio has to choose between a movie star who demands $25 million and an unknown actor who will happily work for $25,000. The famous actor costs a lot more money, but will also bring in a lot more revenue.

It will also be much easier for the studio to market the film and sell tickets and movie merchandise such as DVDs, posters, and other items.

Hiring an unknown actor will help keep the budget low, but it won't get people to buy tickets for movie theaters. So the opportunity cost is higher than if the filmmakers had hired the Hollywood star. Producers know that the right star in the right movie is as good as gold.

INSIDER INSIGHT

"As far as the filmmaking process is concerned, stars are essentially worthless—and absolutely essential."
William Goldman, screenwriter

EARNING POWER

Thousands of talented people work behind the scenes to make a big Hollywood movie. The most important crew member is the director. Directors make all the major creative decisions that shape a film. They have the final word on the cast, sets, music, costumes, and special effects. Directors are involved in every stage of production—and can earn millions for doing so.

Other top earners—for example, art directors, makeup and costume artists, and film editors—help shape the look of a movie. They work closely with the director to design and create the sets, style the actors, and piece the scenes together after filming. The average salary for these crew members is $75,000 to $125,000, but well-known artists make much more.

WHAT DO YOU THINK?

How can the law of supply and demand be used to explain why matinees cost less than evening films? What is the result on ticket prices of fewer people going to the movies during the day?

WANTED

Why do top crew and cast members earn so much money? The answer is **supply and demand**. Supply is how much of something is available. Demand is the willingness and ability of consumers to buy a product or service. When supply is low and demand is high, prices rise. When supply is high and demand is low, prices drop. There are few big-name directors whom studios trust to make their big-budget films. There are few **A-list actors** who bring crowds into theaters. Since the supply of talent is low and the demand for them is high, the stars can name their price—and usually get it.

EXTRA! EXTRA!

Not everyone in Hollywood makes millions of dollars, however. Background actors are the lowest-paid members of a film's cast. They make about $100 a day for playing customers in a restaurant, passengers on a ship, or other non-speaking, background parts. They don't earn a lot of money because demand is low (there is not a vast number of movies being made) and supply is high (there are many struggling actors looking for work). In fact, these actors are so replaceable, they are simply called "extras"!

ABOVE: Stunt drivers take a lot of risks—and take home a lot of money for doing so.

It takes a big crew to make a big Hollywood picture.

ACTION!

REEL COSTS

Each day of filming, the entire cast and crew must be scheduled, directed, housed, and fed. The actors must be costumed and have their hair and makeup done. Sets must be built, dressed (decorated), and lit. State-of-the-art cameras, sound equipment, and other gear must be rented. Stunts must be planned and performed. People and equipment must be moved and set up for each scene. Costs can quickly spiral out of control. Schedules, budgets, and flowcharts must be carefully followed to ensure everything goes as planned.

WHAT DO YOU THINK?

Imagine you had to write a schedule for a day's film shoot and to work out the costs. How would you go about doing this?

Producers must pay fees to stop traffic and close city streets during filming.

THE MOST EXPENSIVE MOVIES EVER MADE

	Release Date	Movie	Budget in U.S. dollars
1	3/9/2012	John Carter	$300,000,000
2	5/25/2007	Pirates of the Caribbean: At World's End	$300,000,000
3	12/13/2013	The Hobbit: There and Back Again	$270,000,000
4	12/14/2012	The Hobbit: An Unexpected Journey	$270,000,000
5	11/24/2010	Tangled	$260,000,000
6	5/4/2007	Spider-Man 3	$258,000,000
7	7/15/2009	Harry Potter and the Half-Blood Prince	$250,000,000
8	5/20/2011	Pirates of the Caribbean: On Stranger Tides	$250,000,000
9	7/20/2012	The Dark Knight Rises	$250,000,000
10	12/18/2009	Avatar	$237,000,000

Each of the top ten most expensive movies ever made cost more than $230 million to make. [Figures are rounded to the nearest million.]

BUDGET BUSTERS

Some types of movies take longer to shoot than others. The longer filming takes, the more money it costs. In epic science-fiction films, such as *John Carter* and *Avatar*, entire worlds must be created by the filmmakers. That takes a lot of time and money. In action-adventure movies, such as *Pirates of the Caribbean* and *The Dark Knight Rises*, fight scenes, car chases, and explosions bring big excitement to the big screen. They also add big bucks to the budget. It can take days to shoot an action sequence that lasts just a few seconds!

Where a movie is filmed also affects its shooting schedule and budget. Some movies are shot on location in the "real world." For example, most scenes in *The Hobbit* movies were filmed in remote areas of New Zealand. It takes time and money to transport the cast and crew to these faraway places. Other films are shot on sound stages. A sound stage is a soundproof building on a studio lot. Transportation costs are lower when films are shot in studios. But huge, complex movie sets require a lot of resources to build.

CUTTING COSTS

STAYING ON BUDGET

Filmmakers are always looking for ways to cut costs and stay on budget. They shoot during the day to avoid renting expensive lights and paying night fees to crews. They steer clear of busy or famous places that charge high location fees. They even cut the pay of producers, directors, and lead actors. But don't worry! The stars get their money in the end.

Film crews start work early in the morning to make the most of the daylight hours.

BASIC ECONOMICS

Studios help cover costs by letting companies advertise products in their films. The companies pay money or give the filmmakers vehicles, computers, or other needed items. In return, the movie characters drive cars, drink sodas, and use products made by the companies.

The Canadian film industry is sometimes called "Hollywood North." Many American movies are shot in Toronto (shown here), Vancouver, and other cities in Canada because they resemble cities in the United States.

MO' MONEY

Many stars trade high salaries up front for a share, or part, of the film's gross revenue. They may get a share of box office sales or a chunk of the movie's overall profits. A film's profits include money earned from other **revenue streams** such as DVD sales, merchandise, and music soundtracks. If the film does well, the stars make even more money than they would have done with hefty salaries alone. Freeing up money in the budget allows the filmmakers to make a bigger and better movie—that in turn earns everyone more money!

ADDED INCENTIVES

Giving stars a share of the profits is an **incentive** for them to make good movies. An incentive is something that motivates a person or business to do something. For example, you might get dessert if you eat your dinner or extra allowance if you do more chores. Ice cream and money are good incentives. What are some other incentives you have at home and school?

Some governments offer filmmakers incentives to shoot movies in their countries. The filmmakers may pay less money in taxes or get cash **rebates** for filming there. They may also save money by hiring local crews and renting cheaper locations. The incentives help filmmakers cut costs and stay on budget. They help foreign countries by bringing in jobs and revenue and growing their film industries.

THAT'S A WRAP!

POST-PRODUCTION

Once a movie has been filmed—or is "in the can" as they say in the movie biz (from the days when rolls of film were stored in flat cans)—post-production begins. Hundreds of hours of footage must be carefully watched and edited. Film editors work long hours cutting and piecing the shots together to tell the story. Visual effects and music are also added to the movie at this stage. It can take months before the final cut is ready for theaters. In fact, post-production usually lasts longer—and costs more money—than shooting the film itself.

TRICKS OF THE TRADE

Composers write winning scores in post-production. A score is all the background music that sets the tone of a film. The score builds suspense in horror movies and triggers tears in dramas. It also makes composers—who can earn a million dollars or more per film—smile all the way to the bank.

A sound engineer mixes a film's dialogue, music, background noise, and sound effects in a sound recording studio.

BASIC ECONOMICS

Although CGI costs millions of dollars, it can also save producers time and money. The technology allows filmmakers to create virtual worlds without building massive sets. It allows them to include huge crowd scenes without hiring armies of extras. Computers have completely changed the way movies are made—and how their budgets are spent.

Visual effects can destroy a film's budget!

VISUAL EFFECTS

The biggest post-production cost for most films is visual effects. Effects—from dinosaurs and monsters to tidal waves and spaceships—can double a film's budget. Big Hollywood studios often spend $100 million or more on computer-generated imagery (CGI) and other effects for a single movie! Remember the list of most expensive films on page 23? Those movies all had huge special effects budgets. It took six years and about $260 million to make the computer-animated film *Tangled*. It took a similar budget and more than 900 special effects shots to get *Spider-Man 3* swinging into theaters.

THE COST OF MUSIC

Music is another sound expense in post-production. Studios pay performers to write and record original songs for movie soundtracks. Famous singers can earn a million dollars for a single song! Buying the rights to popular songs can cost studios even more money. The bigger the hit, the bigger the fee to use the song in a film.

4 BOX OFFICE BUZZ

After millions of dollars are poured into making movies, there is still a lot of work to do—and a lot of money to spend. Studios must get people into theaters so they can start earning back their money. They market their films to get the word out and the moviegoers in.

SAMPLE MARKETING BUDGET

35.5%
TV commercials

4.2%
Theatrical trailers

4.4%
Internet

10.1%
Newspapers

24%
Other media
(magazines, billboards,
radio, cable TV)

21.8%
Other non-media costs
(market research,
publicity, etc.)

About one third of the marketing budget is spent on TV commercials and one fourth on other media.

Social media is a **cost-effective** way to promote films. Facebook, Twitter, and other social media sites can be used to reach people around the world quickly and cheaply. *The Hunger Games* had two million Facebook and Twitter followers 12 weeks before it hit theaters! *John Carter* had only 40,000 Facebook fans—and was a flop.

Kung Fu Panda movies are advertised at a street parade in Times Square, New York City.

MOVIE MARKETING

Studios begin promoting their films long before they hit theaters. They try to create "buzz" that builds up until opening day. Buzz is a feeling of excitement or anticipation about a product or service. Movie marketing usually starts with a theatrical trailer and takes off from there. Studios use TV and radio spots, websites and banner ads, magazine and newspaper ads, billboards and movie posters, and merchandise of all kinds to sell their movies. Since each film is a unique product, each one must be marketed differently. For example, children's films are often advertised at fast food restaurants. You would never see a gruesome character from a horror movie in a Happy Meal!

Although each marketing campaign is unique, they all have one thing in common— they cost a fortune. Studios spend millions of dollars promoting their films. And marketing is not part of a film's budget. If a film cost $200 million to make, it might cost another $100 million—or more—to promote. In fact, marketing can double the overall cost of making a movie! Why do studios spend so much time and money marketing their films?

STAR WARS

Big studios are **monopolistic competitors**. That means they sell products (movies) that are similar to other products but unique in their own way. For example, there are many superhero movies but only one *Iron Man*. There are many animated films but only one *Toy Story*. Because there are similar products in the marketplace, studios must compete for business. They spend big bucks to create buzz and make their movies stand out from the competition.

THE COST OF DISTRIBUTION

Studios spend millions of dollars producing and promoting big-budget films. But the expenses don't end there. They must also distribute the films. It costs about $2,000 for each print, or copy, of a movie. Studios must also pay to make, store, and send the prints to theaters, then to get them back. With about 130,000 movie screens around the world, distribution costs can quickly add up.

In the past, studios released their films in different places at different times. This cut costs because studios could reuse the same prints again and again. Word-of-mouth advertising helped sell the films and reduced marketing costs. Today, movies open at the same time everywhere to combat **piracy**. Piracy is the act of copying and selling films illegally. Studios must pay millions of dollars to release their movies on the same day around the world—or risk losing millions of dollars in ticket sales to piracy.

RISKY BUSINESS

Like all businesses, film studios are always weighing risk versus **reward**. In economics, the higher the risk, the bigger the expected payoff—but the larger the loss if the movie is a flop! The more theaters that show a film, the more tickets can be sold and the more revenue can be made. But if no one wants to see it and the film flops, the studio loses more money if they make and distribute prints to every theater in the country.

DIRECT TO DVD

Studio heads review films carefully to decide how—or if—they want to distribute them. If they think a film will not bring in big numbers at the box office, they may decide to avoid the high costs of promotion and distribution altogether. When that happens, the studio may release the film directly to DVD. Many independent films also go straight to DVD. The filmmakers cannot afford major marketing campaigns and high distribution costs. Independents sometimes sell their films to big studios or make distribution deals with them. The studios market and release the films in select theaters—and take most of the profits for doing so.

BASIC ECONOMICS

Why do movie refreshments cost so much? Theater owners must charge high prices for popcorn, soda, and other snacks to make a profit. It costs them buckets of money to run jumbo theaters and they must share ticket sales with studios. In fact, the movie is a **loss leader** for theaters. A loss leader is a product (like a movie ticket) sold at a low price to draw in consumers—who then buy other more profitable goods (such as popcorn).

3D screens are popping up in theaters everywhere. In 2012, there were 13,559 3D screens in the United States alone.

OPENING WEEKEND

A KEY INDICATOR

Months of hard work and loads of money lead up to the main event: opening weekend in theaters. If the marketing team has done its job well, fans will be lined up around the block to see the hottest stars in the coolest new film. If not, a poor opening weekend can spell disaster for a film. A movie's opening is a key **indicator** of how many people want to see it and how much revenue it will make at the box office. A big opening weekend can indicate big ticket sales—and profits—in the weeks to come.

FLOODING THE MARKET

Sometimes theaters are packed on opening weekend, then deserted in the weeks to follow. Word spreads quickly on the Internet and social media, and bad reviews can quickly ruin a film. Studios flood the market on opening weekends by getting their films into as many theaters as possible. They try to sell a ton of tickets before people hear how good—or bad—the film is.

BIGGEST WEEKENDS AT THE BOX OFFICE—TICKET SALES

#	Date	Film	Ticket Sales
1	May 4, 2012	Marvel's The Avengers	$207,438,708
2	May 3, 2013	Iron Man 3	$174,144,585
3	Jul 15, 2011	Harry Potter and the Deathly Hallows: Part II	$169,189,427
4	Jul 20, 2012	The Dark Knight Rises	$160,887,295
5	Jul 18, 2008	The Dark Knight	$158,411,483
6	Mar 23, 2012	The Hunger Games	$152,535,747
7	May 4, 2007	Spider-Man 3	$151,116,516
8	Nov 20, 2009	The Twilight Saga: New Moon	$142,839,137
9	Nov 16, 2012	The Twilight Saga: Breaking Dawn, Part 2	$141,067,634

These films all made millions of dollars at the box office on their opening weekends.

Popular actors, such as Brad Pitt (right), bring loyal fans to premieres. Films can earn 40 percent of their total gross the first weekend in theaters.

WHAT DO YOU THINK?

Studios often schedule major releases for the holidays and summertime, when people have more free time to go to the movies. They also count on sequels of popular films to bring crowds back into theaters. Look at the chart on the opposite page. How many films were sequels? When were they released? How did these factors reduce the risk for film studios?

STUDIOS CUT A DEAL

Studios often make deals with movie theaters that give the studios 80 to 100 percent of box office sales the first week the film plays. Each week after that, the studio gets a smaller chunk of ticket sales while more money goes to the theater. In general, a studio can count on about half the total revenue earned at the box office.

SMASH HIT OR MONEY LOSER?

Some big-budget films open to huge crowds and become smash hits. They fill theaters for weeks and earn piles of money for the studios. *Avatar* grossed nearly $3 billion in ticket sales around the world! Other films have massive budgets but fail to draw the crowds. *John Carter* cost $300 million to make and lost money in ticket sales. So what makes a hit? That is the multi-million-dollar question that studios try to answer each year.

Major Hollywood studios count on blockbusters to turn profits. Blockbusters are big-budget "event films" that appeal to a wide audience. *Harry Potter, Star Wars,* and the other films in the chart to the right are all blockbusters. They have huge production budgets, mainly due to their state-of-the-art animation and special effects. Studios spend millions selling the films and all the products that go along with them—and it usually pays off.

CHILD'S PLAY

Most blockbusters are geared toward young people because they go to the movies more than anyone else. In 2012, consumers aged 12–24 bought nearly one third of all tickets sold in theaters. Young people often have free time and disposable income. They will line up for days to see a movie when it opens in theaters—then go back to see it again and again. Young people also hang movie posters on their walls, wear T-shirts with film logos on them, and buy other products that tie in with a hit film.

SLEEPERS IN SEATTLE

Not all successful films are instant hits. Some movies gain momentum and ticket sales the longer they play in theaters. These films—called sleeper hits—have much smaller marketing campaigns

INSIDER INSIGHT

"The big-budget blockbuster is becoming one of the most dependable forms of filmmaking."
Peter Jackson, film director

The stars shine brightly on the Hollywood Walk of Fame.

THE MOST PROFITABLE MOVIES (figures in U.S. dollars)

	Release Date	Movie	Budget (U.S. $)	Worldwide Gross	Profit
1	12/18/2009	Avatar	$237,000,000	$2,783,918,982	$1,154,959,491
2	12/19/1997	Titanic	$200,000,000	$1,842,879,955	$721,439,978
3	7/15/2011	Harry Potter and the Deathly Hallows: Part II	$125,000,000	$1,328,111,219	$539,055,610
4	12/17/2003	The Lord of the Rings: The Return of the King	$94,000,000	$1,141,408,667	$476,704,334
5	6/11/1993	Jurassic Park	$63,000,000	$923,863,984	$398,931,992
6	6/15/1994	The Lion King	$79,300,000	$952,880,140	$397,140,070
7	5/19/2004	Shrek 2	$70,000,000	$919,838,758	$389,919,379
8	5/19/1999	Star Wars Ep. I: The Phantom Menace	$115,000,000	$1,006,863,310	$388,431,655
9	5/25/1977	Star Wars Ep. IV: A New Hope	$11,000,000	$797,900,000	$387,950,000
10	6/11/1982	ET: The Extra-Terrestrial	$10,500,000	$792,965,326	$385,982,660

Many blockbuster movies are sequels or part of a successful series. The two most profitable movies ever, however, were stand-alone films.

BASIC ECONOMICS

It's time to do some movie math! If a blockbuster cost $100 million to make and earned $200 million at the box office, and a sleeper hit cost $10 million to make and earned $100 million, which film had a better return on its investment? Why?

than blockbusters do. They rely instead on word-of-mouth advertising. People tell their friends and families about the movies and soon they are surprise hits—with surprisingly big profits. Most sleepers are low-budget independent films that have good **return on investment (R.O.I.)**. That means they make a lot of money relative to the amount it cost to make them. For example, the indie film *Paranormal Activity* had a budget of just $15,000—and grossed nearly $200 million!

5 BEYOND THE BOX OFFICE

Big numbers at the box office can bring in big bucks for movie studios. But even when the film is a success, most studios don't profit from ticket sales. In fact, ticket sales usually make up less than half of a film's overall revenue. The box office is a loss leader for many films. Movies attract thousands of consumers and create fans who later buy other products and services offered by the studios.

INSIDER INSIGHT

"Netflix, Amazon, iTunes—whatever platforms emerge—we are looking at as having the same potential that home video had for the movie business."
Bob Iger, C.E.O. of The Walt Disney Company

Most films make ancillary revenue for about ten years after they are released. Video rentals (above) and in-flight movies (left) help keep the money rolling in long after the movie first appeared in theaters.

THE LOWDOWN ON HIGH PRICES

Why don't studios make more profit from ticket sales? The reason is that production costs have risen dramatically in the past few years, while the price of movie tickets has increased only slightly. If theaters raise ticket prices too much, they will lose consumers. People will no longer be able to afford movie tickets and will spend their money on other products. So studios keep prices low and look for other ways to make **ancillary revenue**.

THE REEL MONEY

Ancillary revenue is money made from goods and services outside a company's main product. For example, some gas stations sell car washes, snacks, and other products besides gas. These sales generate ancillary revenue and help grow the business. Film studios make ancillary revenue from video sales and rentals. Many families have home theaters and choose to watch DVDs or Blu-ray discs on their own big screens instead of going to theaters. Loyal fans buy DVDs so they can watch their favorite films over and over again. For example, more than 7.4 million copies of *The Hunger Games* were sold in 2012. It was the top-selling DVD of the year, earning revenue of more than $123 million.

SELLING THE RIGHTS

Studios also profit by selling the rights to show their films on the small screen. TV networks, pay-per-view stations, and airlines pay top dollar to play top films. Amazon, iTunes, and other online stores buy the rights to sell DVDs and movie downloads. Services such as Netflix pay studios for the rights to stream movies over the Internet.

WHAT DO YOU THINK?

Ticket sales make up only a small portion of a film's revenue. Why don't movie theaters raise their prices so everyone can make more money? What would happen if they did? Would they sell more or fewer tickets? How would that affect their **bottom line**?

Toys from franchises such as *Star Wars* (left) and *Toy Story* (below) give studios big profits to play with.

Woody's ROUNDUP

Hey Howdy Hey!

MONEY FROM OTHER SOURCES

Merchandise sales make up a huge part of a studio's ancillary revenue. Fans flock to stores to buy film soundtracks, posters, and books. They scoop up toys, games, bedding, clothes, backpacks, toothbrushes, and collectibles of all types. For example, the 2006 film *Cars* earned $461 million at the box office. It then made another $10 billion in merchandise sales!

The film studios don't make all the items themselves. Instead, they make deals with manufacturing companies that want to use movie characters and logos for their products. The companies pay **licensing fees** to use the **intellectual property** of the studios. Intellectual property is the original ideas that belong to a certain person or business. In return for the **licenses**, the studios get a share of merchandise sales.

FILM FRANCHISES

Some movies make so much ancillary revenue that they become franchises. A **film franchise** is a series of films with a recognizable **brand** and many related products. The 1977 film *Star Wars* was the first major movie franchise. People poured into theaters to see the film—and then rushed to stores to buy *Star Wars* action figures and lightsabers. Today, *Harry Potter* is the most successful film franchise. The eight *Harry Potter* films have made a total of nearly $8 billion in ticket sales worldwide. And the movie merchandise keeps the studio's profits magically growing.

MOVIE FRANCHISES

Franchise	Number of Movies	Total Worldwide Box Office
Harry Potter	8	$7,709,205,984
Star Wars	7	$4,485,672,683
The Avengers	11	$5,013,935,710
James Bond	24	$6,198,420,185
Batman	11	$3,714,171,639
Shrek	6	$3,547,384,012
Spider-Man	4	$3,254,035,946
Twilight	6	$3,352,322,180
Lord of the Rings	6	$3,952,551,485
Pirates of the Caribbean	4	$3,700,230,282
Star Trek	12	$1,929,055,505
Transformers	3	$2,668,586,367
X-Men	6	$2,255,113,292
Iron Man	3	$2,417,996,729
Indiana Jones	4	$1,983,736,193
Fast and the Furious	7	$2,380,257,787
Toy Story	4	$1,975,515,949
Jurassic Park	4	$2,184,218,798
Superman	8	$1,528,371,608
Mission: Impossible	4	$2,096,122,461

Movie franchises with recognizable brands make billions of dollars for their studios.

TRICKS OF THE TRADE

Film studios spend a lot of time and money on merchandising because they are monopolistic competitors. They compete to win consumers—and they will do anything to make their films stand out. Walt Disney and Universal Studios have theme parks to promote their films.

BACK TO THE FUTURE

What does the future hold for the film industry? Will movies still exist—and still turn profits—in the years to come? Filmmakers everywhere would give anything to answer those questions. Unfortunately, hot-tub time machines and crystal balls only work in the movies. But we can study trends in the industry to predict where it is heading—and how bumpy the ride will be.

STUDIO VERSUS INDEPENDENT FILMS

Year	2003	2004	2005	2006	2007	2008	2009	2010	2011	2012	12 v 11	12 v 03
Films released	455	489	507	594	611	638	557	563	609	677	11%	49%
3D film releases	2	2	6	8	6	8	20	26	45	36	-20%	n/a
MPAA member total	180	179	194	204	189	168	158	141	141	128	-9%	-29%
MPAA studios	102	100	113	124	107	108	111	104	104	94	-10%	-8%
MPAA studio subsidiaries	78	79	81	80	82	60	47	37	37	34	-8%	-56%
Non-members	275	310	313	390	422	470	399	422	468	549	17%	100%

MPAA = Motion Picture Association of America

As the number of movies made by the main studios has gently declined in the last 12 years, the number of independent (non-member) movies has about doubled.

BASIC ECONOMICS

Piracy costs the film industry billions of dollars in revenue each year. People illegally copy and sell movies for next to nothing. Studios cannot compete with those prices—or afford to lose the booty that pirates steal from them.

Pirates might be cool in movies, but pirating movies is not cool at all—or legal.

FALLING WITH STYLE

Movie studios try to make bigger and better films each year. They spend mega bucks on stars and state-of-the-art special effects. They make budget-busting blockbusters, then add sequels. It sounds like a surefire formula for success, right? Wrong! Fewer people go to the movies now than ever before. Today, only about one in ten Americans sees a film in the theater each week. Compare that to 1930, when nearly seven out of ten Americans hit theaters weekly. What has changed?

HOUSTON, WE HAVE A PROBLEM!

Today, there is more competition for the film industry. New technologies—such as big-screen TVs and surround sound—have taken consumers out of movie theaters and put them into home theaters. The Internet, smartphones, Netflix, and countless other technologies have given consumers more options for their free time and disposable income. Other forms of entertainment—from water parks to skate parks—are also available to consumers.

There is more competition within the film industry. The number of studio releases is steadily falling, while independent films are taking a bigger share of the market each year. New technologies—such as 3D effects—raise production costs and limit the number of big blockbusters that Hollywood studios can make.

At the same time, other technologies—such as high-quality video equipment and home computer editing systems—allow more people to make independent films. More films mean more competition, so it gets harder and harder for independents to sell or distribute their movies.

41

THE SHOW MUST GO ON

RISING TICKET SALES

Despite the many challenges facing the film industry, producers keep making movies—and movies keep making money. Despite rising ticket costs, pricey popcorn, and sticky floors, consumers keep coming back to movie theaters. In fact, ticket sales were up six percent in 2012 compared to 2011. Films brought in nearly $35 billion in revenue at the worldwide box office. The business of making movies continues to be one of the most powerful and profitable industries around.

THE GREAT ESCAPE

Movies take you to galaxies far, far away. They send you over the rainbow and make you king of the world—and help you forget your cares for a while.

INSIDER INSIGHT

"This is a time when we need to smile more and Hollywood movies are supposed to do that for people in difficult times."
Steven Spielberg, film director

WORLDWIDE TICKET SALES (approximate)

U.S. & Canada	$10.8b
China	$2.7b
Japan	$2.4b
UK	$1.7b
France	$1.7b
India	$1.4b
Germany	$1.3b
South Korea	$1.3b
Russia	$1.2b
Australia	$1.2b

The United States and Canada still dominate worldwide ticket sales, but China is now second and its sales are on the rise.

New stories, new stars, and new technologies keep consumers coming back to the movies. Familiar faces (such as these Stormtroopers) and favorite franchises (such as *Star Wars*) also draw crowds.

Movies are especially popular when the economy is poor. Remember how many Americans went to the movies in 1930? That was the start of the Great Depression. People everywhere had lost their jobs and homes. They were struggling to feed their families. But somehow they scraped up enough cash to see musicals and comedy films. They sang and laughed and escaped to the magical world of Hollywood.

Today, much of the world is in a recession. A recession is a period of time when business slows and the economy is poor. The recession began in 2007, and ticket sales have been steadily rising ever since. Will they continue to climb? Will the film industry continue to survive the challenges it faces? Only time—or a hot-tub time machine—will tell.

GLOSSARY

A-list actors A list or group of the most desirable and well-known actors in the movie business

ancillary revenue Money made from selling goods or services that are not a company's main product

assets Resources that have value and help producers make money

bottom line Total profits or losses

box office Where tickets are sold; the financial success of a film

brand A name or design that people recognize with a certain product

budget A detailed plan that tracks money coming in and being spent

capital Money that is used to make other products or services

competition Companies fighting to sell their products to consumers

consumers People who buy goods and services

cost-effective Something that earns a lot of money relative to production cost

disposable income Money left over after bills and living expenses are paid

distribute To supply products to businesses that sell them to consumers

economics The study of how goods and services are bought, sold, and used

economy How a country uses its money and resources

film franchise A series of movies with a recognizable brand and products

finance To provide the money needed to make or do something

fixed costs Expenses that do not change regardless of production

gross Total revenue earned before any expenses have been paid

incentive An outcome that influences a decision to buy or do something

indicator Something that shows a trend or direction a business is heading

inflation A rise in the price of goods and services over time

intellectual property Creations or ideas that belong to someone

invest To put money into a company or project in hopes of making a profit

investors People who put money into a company or organization

GLOSSARY

licenses Agreements to use the intellectual properties of others

licensing fees Costs companies pay to use ideas or characters in their products

loss leader A product sold at a loss to generate sales in other areas

market economy A system in which consumers and producers freely make decisions about what to buy and sell

marketing All the forms of advertising used to sell products

market share The portion of total sales earned by one company

monopolistic competitors Companies that sell similar products

monopoly A one-company market

opportunity cost The value of the option that was not chosen

perks Money, goods, or other special benefits an employee is entitled to

piracy The illegal act of copying and selling a film without permission

premium An extra charge added to a regular price

profit Money gained after business expenses have been paid

rebates Refunds on monies paid

return on investment A measure of how much profit an investor has made

revenue Total money received from the sale of goods or services

revenue streams Different ways that companies earn money

reward A profit or return on an investment

rights Permission to use a story

risk The chance of losing money invested in a project or product

salaries Fixed payments made to employees on a regular basis

sequel A film or other work that continues an earlier story

sponsor A business that helps pay costs in exchange for advertising

studio A company that plans, produces, and distributes movies

supply and demand When demand for products drives the supply of products up and down and affects their prices

variable costs Expenses that change when production rises or falls

FIND OUT MORE

BOOKS TO READ

Acton, Johnny and David Goldblatt. *Eyewitness Books: Economy.* Dorling Kindersley, 2010.

Andrews, Carolyn. *What Are Goods and Services?* (Economics in Action). Crabtree Publishing, 2008.

Challen, Paul. *What Is Supply and Demand?* (Economics in Action). Crabtree Publishing, 2010.

Flatt, Lizann. *The Economics of the Super Bowl* (Economics of Entertainment). Crabtree Publishing, 2013.

Girard Golomb, Kristen. *Economics and You, Grades 5-8.* Mark Twain Media, 2012.

Hollander, Barbara. *Money Matters: An Introduction to Economics.* Heinemann Raintree, 2010.

Hulick, Kathryn. *The Economics of a Video Game* (Economics of Entertainment). Crabtree Publishing, 2013.

O'Brien, Lisa. *Lights, Camera, Action!: Making Movies and TV from the Inside Out.* Owlkids Books, 2007.

Perl, Sheri. *The Economics of a Rock Concert* (Economics of Entertainment). Crabtree Publishing, 2013.

WEBSITES

http://dailyinfographic.com
Information of all types presented visually

http://mpaa.org
Facts, figures, and news about the movie industry

www.scholastic.com/browse/collection.jsp?id=455
Articles and activities about the economy

www.socialstudiesforkids.com/subjects/economics.htm
An overview of economics

www.the-numbers.com
Box office data and records

INDEX

REFERENCES

ACKNOWLEDGMENTS

The author wishes to thank the following people for assistance and credit these sources of information:

Interviews

Thought Economics: The Role of Film in Society: Interview with film producer Tom Sherak. http://thoughteconomics.blogspot.ca/2011/06/role-of-film-in-society.html

Industry Reports and Articles

"2012 Theatrical Market Statistics." Motion Picture Association of America.

Acuna, Kirsten. "Movie Studios Are Setting Themselves Up for Huge Losses." *Business Insider*, March 6, 2013.

Broderick, Peter. "The ABC's of No-Budget Filmmaking." *Filmmaker Magazine*, Winter 1992.

Bunting, Glenn F. "$78 Million of Red Ink?" *Los Angeles Times*, April 15, 2007.

Campea, John. "Economics of the Movie Theater—Where the Money Goes and Why It Costs Us So Much." The Movie Blog, October 22, 2007.

Chmielewski, Dawn C. & Rebecca Keegan. "Merchandise sales drive Pixar's 'Cars' franchise." *Los Angeles Times*, June 21, 2011.

"Chronology of Film History." Digital History.

Cieply, Michael. "Global Ticket Sales for Movies Rise 6%." *The New York Times*, March 21, 2013.

Clements, Blayne. "Law of Supply and Demand Is Not Always Followed in Business." Clarksville Online, March 17, 2010.

Davidson, Adam. "How Does the Film Industry Actually Make Money?" *The New York Times*, June 26, 2012.

Denby, David. "Has Hollywood Murdered the Movies?" *New Republic*, September 14, 2012.

Epstein, Edward Jay. "Hollywood's Real Money Machine." *Wall Street Journal*, March 4, 2010.

Epstein, Edward Jay. "How to Finance a Hollywood Blockbuster." *Slate*, April 25, 2005.

"Film Industry by the Numbers." Daily Infographic, October 27, 2010.

"Hollywood by the Numbers." The Smoking Gun, February 27, 2006.

"Infographic: product placement in the movies." Blame It on the Voices, November 24, 2011.

Menand, Louis. "Gross Points: Is the blockbuster the end of cinema?" *The New Yorker*, February 7, 2005.

Mehta, Stephanie N. "The future of Hollywood: Money men." *Fortune*, May 23, 2006.

Morris, Ben. "Blockbuster economics: So you want to make a movie?" *BBC News*, May 7, 2012.

Pautz, Michelle C. "The Decline in Average Weekly Cinema Attendance: 1930–2000." *Issues in Political Economy*, 11 (Summer): 54–65, 2002.

Pomerantz, Dorothy. "Robert Downey Jr. Tops Forbes' List of Hollywood's Highest-Paid Actors." *Forbes*, July 16, 2013.

Porter, Eduardo & Geraldine Fabrikant. "A Big Star May Not a Profitable Movie Make." *The New York Times*, August 28, 2006.

Rose, Lacey. "Hollywood's Most Expensive Movies." *Forbes*, December 18, 2006.

Susman, Gary. "We call it martian accounting." *The Guardian*, August 31, 2001.

"The 10 Most Expensive Movies of All Time." Know Your Money, November 5, 2008.

"The Cost of Making a Hollywood Movie." Anomalous Material, March 26, 2010.

"The Economic Contribution of the Motion Picture & Television Industry to the United States." Motion Picture Association of America.

"The Film Business Today." CyberCollege, April 6, 2012.

Thomas, Archie. "Anatomy of a blockbuster." *The Guardian*, June 11, 2004.

Thompson, Derek. "The 6 Graphs You Need to See to Understand the Economics of Awful Blockbuster Movies." *The Atlantic*, July 10, 2013.

Troy, Castor. "Are Actors Overpaid?" *MovieFanFare*, May 5, 2010.

"Types of Content Theft." Motion Picture Association of America.